Mindset Of An Entrepreneur: Fulfil your Potential and Think Like an Entrepreneur

The Marketing Guy

The Marketing Guy
Mindset of an Entrepreneur: Fulfill your Potential and Think like an Entrepreneur

© 2015, The Marketing Guy

ALL RIGHTS RESERVED. This book contains material protected under International and Federal Copyright Laws and Treaties. Any unauthorized reprint or use of this material is prohibited. No part of this book may be reproduced or transmitted in any form or by any means, electronic or mechanical, including photocopying, recording, or by any information storage and retrieval system without express written permission from the author / publisher.

Table Of Contents

Introduction

Chapter one: Standing in your own way

Chapter Two: How many entrepreneurial traits do you have? Quiz

Chapter Three: The Employee Mindset

Chapter Four: Fear

Chapter Five: Work Book

Conclusion

More Books by the Author

Your FREE Bonus

As a way of saying thank you we would like to give you a free bonus for purchasing this book.

You can receive our free Marketing toolkit! The Marketing toolkit includes free money making eBooks, a business start-up checklist and free videos among many, many other things.

The Marketing toolkit is worth hundreds of dollars so make sure you <u>download your FREE bonus</u>

www.themarketingguy.net/subscribe

Some of the things you will learn and get from the Marketing toolkit are:

- Increasing your Productivity skills
- How to get more done
- Develop a killer mindset that will make you think like a successful entrepreneur
- How to create your own successful business
- Create excellent content that stands out and brings you tons of traffic.
- How to create multiple sources of income that you can profit from each month
- And much more!

www.themarketingguy.net/subscribe

Introduction

Imagine, you want to follow the trend that has brought so many to the top of the earning charts. You know it isn't for everyone but you wonder—do I have what it takes? You look at pictures of the great entrepreneurs of our day—Steve Jobs—Donald Trump—Bill Gates. These icons leave you quaking in your boots. But I'm just me... just some guy or gal that works in an office. I'm sick of it but the last thing I need is to start something that fails!

Your heart races, you feel faint as you think of what will become of you when you tell your friends and family "I want to quit my job and become the next great entrepreneur" Their laughter deafens you inside your own head and you just can't bare it. You know those around you too well and you can just hear the condescending conversation. Yes dear, sure you will, we have faith in you. As your Aunty Molly turns to your mother and whispers, "I think it's just a phase—it's going to pass—don't worry".

If this is your scenario whether real or imagined, it's OK, we've got your back. We understand what you're going through. But you know what? It's a good sign—it's a sign from the entrepreneurial gods that fate is on your side. Are we crazy? Didn't you just get through explaining the nervous breakdown you've been having just fantasizing about becoming an entrepreneur and humiliating yourself in front of friends and family? DIDN'T YOU!! Yes, we heard your thoughts loud and clear. And we have great news for you!

This is probably exactly the way it's gonna go down! Aren't you thrilled? We'll wait until someone picks you up off the floor.

OK, better now? Oh, we're sorry, you really thought we were going to hear all that neurosis and tell you that you were just being silly and that everyone around you is going to pat you on the back and sing He/she's a jolly good fellow. And in fact, they'll be lined up at the door to hand you your capitol for the very first startup as an entrepreneur!

You live in a fantasy camp. But we want to make sure you are as successful so we've started this book, in the section marked '*introduction*' to '*introduce'* you to the reality that entrepreneurs face... daily...

In the following chapters you will find the simplicity that does exist to changing your mindset to a successful entrepreneurs mindset.

We call it simple because it's more about your personal choice than anything else. That's right, we will give you the aspect and elements you need to repattern your thinking into a strong leading entrepreneur. Everyone makes this complicated, there is no need!

If you would like more information on how to create a positive mindset and create a business that will love I suggest you check out www.themarketingguy.net

Without further ado let's get started.

Chapter One

Standing In Your Own Way

If you've read any author worth their salt that has written articles and e books about the mindset of entrepreneurs they would have told you this. And if not, we are going to tell you now.

The only force that stands in your way of your own entrepreneurial success is you.

No matter how you cut it guys it's all on you. We have a very picky universe. We know a lot more about the things the past entrepreneurs knew and that is--"What you think about, you bring about". Think that's a bunch of metaphysical woo woo? Well, it's the belief that the successful 1% is aware of.

Call it woo woo, call it quantum physics, call it what you will—it's all about you and what you put out there as a mindset. It rules what action you will take to achieve what you just set your mind to and it will give you the resilience you need to topple the opinions of those around you. It is the only way to win.

The Greats!

So, you walk in a daze wishing you were like all the greats? And how would that be?

Let's see, why not wish you were like one of the greatest men in history and one who is still talked about and revered around the world today? Got a clue? And let's ask this before we unmask him to you. What do you think the greats were like when they started?

Let's see:

- Smarter than everyone around them.
- Richer than everyone around them.
- Handsomer or prettier than everyone around them.
- Backed up and loved by every parent, lover, spouse, teacher, professor, boss etc..
- Just plain popular straight A students right?

Um... No, nada, WRONG!

In fact, most of the first entrepreneurs and geniuses that made great, world-changing discoveries would be, by even today's standards LOSERS!

So, who is this first example? Germany's own Albert Einstein. Yes the discoverer of this small insignificant thing called the theory of relativity or better known as E=MC2. And the bomb that wiped out Hiroshima.

He is our first example because he had a mindset that brought him to where he was. Here was some of his qualities and situations.

Good old Albert was:

- Dyslexic: This is a disorder of the brain by which someone will perceive letters backwards. This doesn't make things easy to read so this brings us to the next bullet point.
- He stunk when it came to science and other subjects but excelled in math. You would think that someone couldn't invent a hydrogen bomb that stunk at science.
- Didn't even start talking until he was 2 and asked his mother why his sister didn't have wheels. Hmm... No comment.
- He was married like three times and one of those times being his cousin.
- He was rejected from colleges yet turned down the offer to be president of Israel.

This man didn't even begin to succeed until his later life! So, what was the one thing that kept him going? Well, we could give the lame answer and say he had a win win and can do attitude, blah blah blah, you get that with every Crackerjack entrepreneurial book. But, that isn't us. You're reading this to get into the mindset of an entrepreneur and though he was more of an inventor and discoverer, Uncle Albert had the heart and mind of an entrepreneur.

Why? Because as he said in one of his most famous quotes " A clever person solves a problem, a wise person avoids it". So what does this mean to the entrepreneurial mindset? Aren't you supposed to run headlong and tackle problems?

Well, not really. An entrepreneur will find ways to avoid a problem that they can't fix and think outside the box to find the resources to go around it. Therefor it is no longer an obstacle. The man that invented the H-bomb HAD TO think as an entrepreneur should think when they approach any obstacle.

So thank you Uncle Albert for the rule of the entrepreneurial mindset number one:

Think Outside the Box! And be unconcerned with the opinions of Others about who you are and where you are going.

So, now we know that thinking outside the box is an important thing, and must be coupled with not being concerned with what others think of you—because you can't do one without the other. We go on to the other guy. Mark Zuckerberg. Most people will either love him or hate him—think he cares? With Facebook worth over 200 Billion. So, did it walk right up to him and fall in his lap? NO, did he freak out and sell FB to the first person that offered this kind of money? Nope, the last we checked he is still the owner and living it large while the rest of us are still moaning about our mediocre lives on FB taking selfies and the millionth picture of our dog.

What was his mindset? Well, apart from sharing a mindset with Albert Einstein in entrepreneurial mindset number one—he had confidence. This boy walked away from Microsoft, and MTV as well as several other major conglomerates that weren't offering him chump change for this invention. He walked away from millions and billions. His people must have thought he lost his mind. But, no, he learned young to negotiate with one hand on the door and be confident.

The mindset of an entrepreneur can be fickle. We will tell you that, like Zuckerberg, you should keep your eyes on the prize and once you have a price or a goal you shouldn't budge, even if the offer sounds great. Then we would tell you that the entrepreneurial mindset embraces change.

OK, so thank you Zuck for the entrepreneurial mindset rule number two.

Embrace change, only when it meets your needs. Stand your ground confidently.

This leads into the third entrepreneurial rule of thumb and our last example Donald Trump.

This is one of the most famous real estate moguls we have in the world with a net worth of 4 billion dollars as of September of 2014. He has the first two rules pretty down pat and more.

He listens to his gut and not to much more. So, you're thinking, he has years of experience on me, of course he can trust his gut! Not a thing to do with it. Yes experience is always good but entrepreneurs are fresh and new and out there with young blood and boundless energy—that is—if you want to be successful. So, you need to get out of your own way! You can take advice but do it the way Darling Donald would, only from those you respect! If your gut tells you a startup is going to be a success and you don't stop your first thought with fear then it will succeed and if it is your first one, make sure you are starting small so you can get out quick. Remember entrepreneurial mindset rule two—embrace change when it meets your needs.

Following your gut is one of the most important rule that Donald has followed consistently through his entrepreneurial career. He has also embraced diversity in his businesses. He is into everything from wealth creation systems to vitamin supplements and much more than his mainstay, real estate. His other trait is tenacity.

And I quote him as stating, "Anyone who thinks my story is even close to over is sadly mistaken.

This is a mindset from a man who learned from an old school generation. But he emerged from that a cutting edge entrepreneur when he developed the mindset that he can be involved in more than one venture whether or not they are all a shining success. And not all of these ventures have been. But, he made them work for him and his bottom line and he also understands that these are learning experiences. You are probably thinking, "He's still learning"? Oh yes and that my friends is another mindset to really sink your teeth into. There is never a time that you stop learning as an entrepreneur.

You see, try to get this before we move on because it's one of the most important parts of this book.

Entrepreneurship is ever changing. The only thing evergreen about entrepreneurship is change—that's it. Of you don't learn what the trends are then you fail—simple as that. This is why we are lending the wisdom of the mindsets of the great entrepreneurs of our time and before. Because they have mastered this understanding. So another warm thank you from Donald Trump for providing the entrepreneurial mindset number three: **Go with your gut and take advice, only from those you respect. Allow yourself to be diverse in your business dealings without fear of failure.**

Chapter Two

How Many Entrepreneurial Traits Do You Have?

OK, so, we thought we would make this a little fun for you. Now that we scared you with the three rules of thumb you are comparing yourself to—we thought we would rub a little salt in the wounds and make you do one of the things entrepreneurs need to do every day. Look at yourself! Yes, it's a fabulous, mindset actually. You have to know how to look at yourself with resolute honesty and shift your attitude according to what serves you best.

So, here is a little 15 question quiz. We urge you to answer the questions thoroughly. After all, you are only hurting yourself by rushing. Then we will address all 15 answers so you can see how to improve yourself and see where you need to be.

Entrepreneurial Self Test

Questions on this quiz will be measured on a scale of 1 to 10. 1 being very low and 10 being very high. You can print this part of the book off or conversely, you can use a separate sheet of paper—just make sure it's all numbered properly. Now, before we begin, you should be aware that this is not a pass or fail exam.

Ewe that's a dirty word! No this is a self-test, which is meant to show you where you are and where you can improve in the traits of a successful entrepreneur.

Questions

On A Scale Of 1-10

1. **How much drive and passion and energy do you have?**

   _____
   _____
   _____
   _____

2. **What are your views on taking responsibility?**

   _____
   _____
   _____
   _____

3. **What is your take on long term commitment?**

   _____
   _____
   _____
   _____

4. **How strong is your belief in yourself?**

   _____
   _____

5. How persistent are you?

6. How well do you set goals?

7. Do you possess the ability to take risks?

8. What use do you make of feedback?

9. **Do you have self imposed standards?**

_____
_____
_____
_____

10. **Can you work under pressure and an element of uncertainty?**

_____
_____
_____
_____

11. **How good is your control of cash flow and other business systems?**

_____
_____
_____
_____

12. **How well do you learn from failures?**

13. Do you use money as a means of keeping score?

14. How well do you deal with delayed gratification?

15. How intelligently do you use your resources?

Addressing The 15 Core Traits

If you haven't taken the quiz yet—DO NOT peek at this section. You'll be doing yourself a great disservice! OK, now that we've hopefully answered all the 15 questions with resolute honesty—we can now address these qualities.

So, why did we choose these particular qualities? We chose these because they are the ones which—when focused upon and adopted—will steer you towards the entrepreneurial mindset. Also, at the end of this book is a workbook that will assist you on a daily basis to work through your challenges in changing you mindset into the sharp mindset of a successful entrepreneur.

Quiz Breakdown

This is the simple part. We simply give you where your score should be and the definition of what each part should be in its ideal state. This is what you need to work up to if your score was a 5 and below. If it's a 6 or higher—less maintenance is needed.

1. **Passion and Energy:** *"Without passion you don't have energy, without energy, you have nothing" Warren Buffet.* Most entrepreneurs do not live a leisurely lifestyle. They are full of passion that makes them so to bed late and wake up early. Though a work-life balance is essential to happiness—the passion you have may drive you forward too much.

2. You will, balance it in time—but just having the feeling that you are happy to be this driven is a sign of a successful entrepreneurial mindset.

3. **Claiming Responsibility:** *"Sometimes when you innovate you make mistakes, It's best to admit them quickly and get on with improving your other innovations"* Steve Jobs. Another essential mindset of entrepreneurs is a responsibility oriented one. It means you can easily claim responsibility for failures and not your employees or partners and quickly find a solution.

4. **Commitment:** *"If I make a commitment to something I will stick with it no matter what"* This is also an essential trait you will see in EVERY successful entrepreneur you will meet. Yes, you embrace change as we stated in chapter one but, this doesn't mean you flux in and out of commitment easily. It means you analyze first what you need to do to get around and avoid a problem. You should be thinking outside the box first, remember Albert Einsteins' take on that in chapter one.

5. **Belief in the Self:** *"You're nuts and you should be proud of it, stick with what you believe in"* Trip Hawkins As an entrepreneur you will be looking for venture capitalists to invest in you. This trait will be something they look for before they roll a red penny toward you. This is often mistaken as arrogance to some. But you aren't—you are just focused on what you believe in and know you can do it.

6. **The Art of Persistence:** *"Nothing in the world can take the place of persistence. Nothing is more common than unsuccessful men with talent. The world is full with educated derelicts. Persistence and determination alone are omnipotent."* – Ray Kroc This is something

your venture capitalists would look at to be coupled with number four. Why? Ask yourself this—would you give millions to someone who believes in themselves but loses persistence at the first sign of struggle? Would you put your money in a bank account that earns no interest? Neither would they. Every Tom, Dick and Harriett out there wants money for something. Prove you aren't one of the masses. Prove your uniqueness.

7. **Set Goals and Aim High:** *"I intend to be, the richest man in the world."* – Howard Hughes. We will give you fair warning that the word 'intend' is a very powerful one. In the next chapter we will get into this a bit more. Setting goals and at least the first steps it will take to achieve them is a seriously important thing. The only way you'll achieve the goals you have—is to marry this one mindset snugly with the first five. The secret to doing this well is to set high goals that challenge your every faculty—but—are realistic and attainable. Above all—make sure they are crystal clear.

8. **Risk Taking:** *"You must take risks, both with your own money or with borrowed money. Risk taking is essential to business growth."* – J. Paul Getty In order for your business to stand the test of time, you need to takes risks that are calculated. This means you are taking risks that are not aimless. They should be aimed toward an end result that suites your company vision.

9. **Using Feedback Intelligently:** *"Sometimes, I think my most important job as a CEO is to listen for bad news. If you don't act on it,*

your people will eventually stop bringing bad news to your attention and that is the beginning of the end." – Bill Gates. No one likes bad news and there are some entrepreneurs that are way too arrogant to listen to any of it. Or, they sift through it strategically to weed out what they don't want to react to. When there is too much ego attached, there is a danger that you will eventually lose your street cred. Listen to and act on feedback, negative or positive in a balanced and intelligent way. That doesn't mean you ask how high when those who disagree with your practices ask you to jump. It means to react to the intelligence of those providing that feedback. In simpler terms, take it from where it comes but leave arrogance at the door.

9. Setting your own standards: *"It takes 20 years to build a reputation and only five Minutes to ruin it. If you think about that, you will do things differently." – Warren Buffett* You have to set your own immoveable standards and stand by your principles. This is not a quality that is seen in business as often as it should. This is another way to prove your uniqueness.

10. Know how to work under pressure and stress: *"You must not only learn to live with tension, you must seek it out. You must learn to thrive on stress." – J. Paul Getty* Many of the famous entrepreneurs that we mentioned in chapter one were in heavy personal debt.

But, they kept their cool and worked their way out of it. Get yourself used to the fact that their will be stress and for practice—seek it out and develop the mindset that you will keep your sensibilities while you think outside the box and work your way out of it all.

11. Internal Control: *"In order to be a player on the fast track, you will need to have a plan on how to gain more and more control. On the fast track, it is control more than money that counts." – Rich Dad* This is another essential watch mindset of potential investors and entrepreneurs alike. If you want to be invested in—then you have to prove that you can control your cash flow and other resources.

12. Intelligent Use of Resources: *"IKEA people do not drive flashy cars or stay at luxury hotels." – Ingvar Kamprad* Sometimes you are in need to build on a tight budget. This is normal. You always have resources around you to utilize—a lack of resources is normally not the issue—a lack of intelligent use of them is.

13. Learning from Failures: *"Failure is just a resting place. It is an opportunity to begin again more intelligently." – Henry Ford* The mindset that a failure is a gift of learning is one that you must possess to be the best at what you do as an entrepreneur. As we mentioned in chapter one—you will have at least one failed endeavor—at least in-part. This is normal and if you spend so much time arrogantly guarding yourself from failure under the guise of perfection—you will have greater failures. This never works.

14. Use Money to "Keep score of where they're at" : *I don't make deals for the money. I've got enough much more than I'll ever need. I do it to do it." – Donald Trump* Once an entrepreneur makes money and hits the first goal. They use that as a milestone. Then they are more than happy to make another milestone to produce their next said amount. Even if that means reinvesting a well thought out portion of that first milestone.

15. Gratification Delay: *"You know you are on the road to success if you would do your job and not get paid for it." – Oprah Winfrey* This is one of those mindsets that not many have. But, if you end up doing something and know in your heart you would do it for free—you are doubly blessed and on your way to success. Entrepreneurial mindsets are not to be tainted with a get rich quick attitude. Some entrepreneurs will work free in-part at first if they know it will build business and reputation.

We hope you scored well for yourself. But, even if you are a fledgling entrepreneur that is still yet feeling their wings and gaining the mindset they need as well as clearing out old bad habits—you have still done well. In the end, to sum up this chapter with a *'spiritual biography'* of sorts, we will marry all 15 of the traits into bio form.

This is not intended for you to use as your professional biography, but to keep as your *'spiritual biography'*. It will help your brain pull together the mindsets into a neat compilation of how you should describe yourself to yourself.

You can also cut it out or copy and paste it somewhere and hang it in places so you an absorb the content.

My Spiritual Entrepreneurial Bio

I _____ am an entrepreneur that is full of **energy and passion.** I have a keen ability to **take responsibility**, and have a love for making and keeping **long standing commitments.** I have a **strong belief in self** which fuels my **persistence** and **goal setting** mindsets. I am impressed by my ability to **take risks**, and my **intelligent use of feedback.** I have **self imposed standards** which are unshakable. I am highly confident in **working under pressure**. I have a uniquely strong **sense of inner control** and **use my resources intelligently.** I **learn from failures** and **make money the** score card of the success of my milestones. But, most of all, I **embrace delayed gratification**. I would do what I do for free, if I was blessed with all the money I needed today.

I am the entrepreneur...

Chapter Three

Out With The Old—In With The New

Recap: Before we start cleaning house—a recap will help you to understand where we were and where we are going with the next chapter. We want this to be as comprehensive as possible so we are on the same page.

In chapter one, we took some examples from a genius and two entrepreneurs. This was to bust any myths we have—and so many of us do—about what type of background and process an entrepreneur is supposed to come from. We saw the shocking decisions and failures as well as learning disabilities and more. Then, in chapter two, we covered the 15 core mindsets that have to be present in order for an entrepreneur to win. We then asked you, in a quiz, to make your own resolutely honest assessment of your own entrepreneurial mindsets. Once we got you clear on those, we married the 15 core mindsets into a biography of the perfect entrepreneur.

Now, where we take you in chapter three will be to clear away the old hindering belief systems you have that according to the results of your self assessment in the quiz, may be holding you back.

For example. You may have scored below a 5 in the area of confidence and this could be due to something only you know. But, we can in fact help everyone regardless of the personal reasons each reader has.

How? Because there are core fundamental reasons for scoring low points on any of the questions. They are the basis of what's behind most of your personal reasons for scoring low. In this way, we can help you clear away these issues and work through them later on in the work book.

Core Fundamental Blockages

There are several core fundamental reasons or blockages that will cause you to not master the mindsets of an entrepreneur.

1. **The Employee Mindset**
2. **Fear Of:**

The reason for their only being two here is that apart from the employee mindset—fear covers everything from lack of confidence to lack of funding etc. It is the largest blanket term which will cover all the reasons for not getting into the mindset that you need to be a successful entrepreneur. So here, we will teach you ways to clear out those blockages and come to a place to start developing your mindset for success.

Leaving the Corporate Employee Mindset Alone:

We all know the corporate world and how it works. It sucks you in while your a young blood and have those delusions of what it's going to be like. Then, in come the threats of constant layoffs, ridiculous performance requests and of course the salary trap. The more they pay that's not hourly—the more they need you to belong to them—to be at their mercy. Then along comes miss sweet pants that will work for less, is younger and is more moldable. Out ya go! This is the employee mindset that must be made in an effigy of some sort and burned. Burned so your subconscious gets it and gets it good that this is no longer who you are.

How to transition from employee mindset to entrepreneur:

It's no good just telling you that this is what you need to do. It has to be shown. And we want you to know first—before we begin—that it's OK if it's a slow process. This is a major shift between two mirror opposites. So, if you get a little stuck, that's OK, that's why we gave you a work book to take you through it daily.

Controlling Your Destiny:

One great way of making the transition is telling yourself that you are controlling your own destiny. Entrepreneurs want nothing to do with surrendering their control to someone else. This is what you do when you belong to the corporate world. Give yourself the truth and state it to yourself like this.

"I want and deserve the kind of lifestyle I have always dreamed of in my retirement. I won't get it slaving away at a job I can't stand and

worse yet—making someone else money. All I'm getting out of working for a corporation is stress which will cause me health problems which will prevent me from living that life"

Can't get much clearer than that can we boys and girls? In time, if you keep this near you—it will push you on.

But, alas, words can only do so much. You have to decide for you that updating that resume and looking for yet another corporate position isn't going to do! Once you've hit rock bottom is when this happens. But it's not entirely your fault. You've been taught to believe by parents, teachers, and the world that working for a company is the surest thing—you may be miserable—but you'll be secure. Really? Tell the people who sunk a lifetime working for GE that one and see how it flies. But again, you are probably thinking out of fear which is the next point we'll cover shortly.

So, the last point on the employee mindset is remembering this.

You miss 100 percent of the shots you never take. – Wayne Gretzky

Look, if you weren't at least playing with the idea, you wouldn't be reading this book. So, let's make a deal. No one says you have to be quitting jobs to go headlong into an entrepreneurial adventure. You can follow the next tips to help transition into the right mindset.

1. **Examine Self Imposed Barriers:** Most people will tell

themselves that no one would want their idea or the most popular negative self-talk, that you could never make money doing whatever you love. It's like we have this barrier to understanding that you can make plenty of money doing what you love. It takes structure and a plan

2. **Use your Present Job as an Example:** The founder of your company is no better a human than you are. So, why not go ahead and take some of the model of your now company and take notes. Now, we aren't telling you to go and steal proprietary information and have a law suit. But, you can certainly learn what to do and what not to do.

3. **Embrace all the Resources you Have:** Feel the fear and do it anyway! Look at ways you can take some time off. Do you have FMLA? Every western country has some kind of family leave that they have to grant you after a years service. Find out how to take advantage of that because they have to at least hold your job and in some cases pay you. This may give you an added layer of security so you can start to learn how to be an entrepreneur. Then you can gently start to think like one, and believe me—it will still be a bit scary but it will be that much harder to go back!

4. **Commitment:** To really think like an entrepreneur, you have to really make sure you are ready to take on more hours.

You have to attend to all the little details and then, look at the big picture at all times. If this is something you're ready to do then great you are half way there. If not, then working a bit more on your fears may help you.

5. **Stop Believing Old School Junk:** Example? You have to work hard for money. If you work hard and prove yourself there is a reward. Um.. actually, you're lucky you get a gold watch.

6. **Change your Attitude About Money:** With an employee mindset, money is something someone gives you in exchange for your contracted services at a rate they normally decide and control.

7. **Learn to Love Numbers:** When you are an employee, the only concern you have is well, maybe how your personal sales were. The CEO has to worry about the cash flow. It may only be the difference to whether you get a bonus or whether you get a promotion or keep our job. How stressful! But, what about when you're an entrepreneur? It's all on you, that's not stressful? Yes but in a hurts so good sort of way. It's what keeps you challenged and your mind and ideas fresh.

8. **Money is Why you Work:** You'll see eventually as you slip into entrepreneur mode, that this philosophy doesn't work. You'll soon see that taking risks and reinvesting money is soon to replace it. When you're an entrepreneur you are essentially a natural risk taker and you learn to love it. As an employee you are actually taught to play it safe in the field and lye low. Here there are uncharted waters to explore.

9. **Outcomes are All on You:** You can bet that your decisions as an employee may weigh upon you in some way. You may even be fired as a result of them or forfeit a raise or a promotion. But, as an entrepreneur you have to start thinking of the outcomes of your

actions being all on you. It can mean your business. And blaming an employee or partner doesn't wash. So, you have to take the grown up view on entrepreneurial life.

10. Develop Short and Long Term Thoughts: When you are an employee, your only task is to make sure you follow directives and take care of what must be done now. When you shift into entrepreneur mode, you have to look at the short term and how the tasks needing fulfillment will affect the future.

11. Getting Used to Discomfort: If you are uncomfortable then you are well underway to becoming a star entrepreneur as long as you don't let it paralyze you. You have to act on an idea especially if it seems risky—try it—you'll be surprised at your results. Your gut that we spoke about in subsequent chapters is what we're talking about here. Once you learn how to differentiate between your gut instinct and fear you'll have it mastered.

12. Learning is Evergreen: As an employee, you come onto the job with a specific skill set and learn to fulfill a limited amount of responsibility. As an entrepreneur you are constantly learning and reinventing.

You learn many different skills. You may not want to do them all and nor will you be good at everything. But, this means you can actually make an executive decision to outsource to someone else the things you won't do. Remembering to keep it cost effective and if you can't then learn it yourself. Because in this game—there is no excuse.

13. You don't have a Vacation from your Business: You will soon learn that when you do have things that need to be done and nobody to outsource it to—you can't take a sick day and let it go to Tom or Sandy and come back having it all done! No, the task at hand awaits you and even if you outsource, it's not like handing it over to a fellow employee and letting the boss oversee the result. You have to track the result of the person who did the job. This can be another headache. The outsourcing world is not a highly professional one depending on where you go. Big mistakes and sub par communication can rule this arena so you need to be extra vigilant.

14. Love what you Do: As an employee you can stick out a job you hate for the benefits and salary, but, as an entrepreneur you are the one at the helm and you'll want to work on the business not 'in' it. You are at the helm of that baby and you'll want to love it to have the energy to put the hours into it that it deserves.

15. Break Rules: As an entrepreneur you enjoy doing things differently, you are always thinking your way around something. As an employee, this behavior could mean your job. Make sure you aren't still afraid to take the leap.

16. Set up a Business Now: It takes a while to actually internalize and habituate a different way of thinking. Start a small business now while you are still working and make a smoother transition while you are waiting it out. When you start thinking like a true entrepreneur you will start to be more itchy to get out of your current job and jump in!

Chapter Four: Core Fundamental Blockage Two-Fear

So we've given you 16 examples of the first core fundamental blockage to becoming an entrepreneur and that is the employee mindsets. Now, we will address the bigger one—fear.

So, what are the typical fears of and employee who wishes to change their mindset to an entrepreneurial mindset? These are all quite personal depending on the different variables there are.

Common Fears of Emerging Entrepreneurs:
1. Failures
2. Funding
3. Lack of Support
4. Lack of Education
5. Image & Lifestyle
6. Experience
7. Youth
8. No Investors
9. Product Not Finished
10. Needing to be Perfect

OK these ten elements are all common fears brought up by budding entrepreneurs. You should actually Google some of the interviews with new entrepreneurs because some of the things they say about how they live and how totally inexperienced they are will make you far less afraid.

This is because you'll know that you are not alone and you don't need to fear half the crap you do. It's all in your head. Tell that to my bank account I just over drew! Oh, come on now, you really are deluding yourself if you think that half the entrepreneurs alive have all this padding behind them. Let's address these fears here and you'll laugh your arses off.

1.   Failures: Think about this for a minute. Don't you think that there will be a conversation about failure and what if's all the damn time? Forget about entrepreneurial stuff—think about anything. You can appeal to your reptilian, irrational mind and drum up at least five ways to fail. One thing is guaranteed, and that is, you'll fail if you really want to. Self-fulfilling prophecy's come cheap and easy like a French whore. So, if you fail EVERY time it down to the altitude of your attitude. But rest assured, you will fail at some of your ideas. The challenge is to learn from it and move on like Steve Jobs advised in chapter one.

2. **Funding:** Most entrepreneurs, including the ones we mentioned in chapter two started out in debt. Way in there! Deep in the forest of almost on the street. In fact, some slept in their cars unbeknown to their clients. You don't have to start with anything but an idea and move from there with calculated risk. Got a family to think about? Not an excuse.

3. As we said in the last section about the core fundamental blockage one—the employee mindset—start while you're still employed. Look into grants—even small ones to get you started.

4. **Lack of Support:** We all want the support of family and friends but at the end of the day—it's the plight of the entrepreneur to stand alone. It's time to prove it I guess. But if you waste energy trying to convince someone that you're doing the right thing—you'll be too depleted of energy to run your business.

5. **Lack of Formal Education:** Street wise with a little formal education is what makes a great entrepreneur. You can learn to sell snowballs to an Eskimo without an MBA and yes MBA's are overrated and unnecessary. People who tell you otherwise only want to justify a lot of money and time for not much more than a credential to hang on the wall. But street cred is what counts. Don't get us wrong, in all seriousness, it's great to have formal education in your professional bio. But if you don't have it—don't be afraid of it and get your arse moving.

6. **Image and Lifestyle:** Oh my God! I'm still living with my mother! I take the tube and can't afford a car. If my clients find out I'm dead. That's BS! This is the old school stuff you were fed. You also don't need to join the country club and learn how to play golf to entertain the clients either! Today, we have way too many different people with different causes in life. You can always use your supposed handicaps to your advantage. You can use having no car as being Green. You can use living with your mother as an investment in your future home. But, you can also keep your big trap shut until or if someone says something.

7. **Experience:** Whether you are in a selling situation or in a teaching situation, you don't need the hands on experience to BS your way through it. It takes more research and practice but you can do it.

8. **Youth:** So you're 22 and wet behind the ears. You still have all the energy and creativity, including thinking outside the box that your aging counter parts are coming into short supply of.

9. **Lack of Investors:** You don't need them. Period. Not everyone has their first idea as a million dollar idea and you shouldn't have to worry either. This may come in time but not every successful entrepreneur had investors. Start small, practice and move ahead.

10. **Having to be Perfect:** The best thing about being an entrepreneur is not having to be perfect. You are expected to make mistakes and learn from them.

So, we've basically cut through all the excuses and fears that you can possibly make. We've covered every dynamic you could have that you can use to block you future as an up and coming entrepreneur. Now, all you have left is to do it. To switch that mind set.

Chapter five is a workbook that we've put together so you can do some daily exercises in the same time frame it takes you to learn a new habit.

Chapter Five: Work Book
Change Your Mindset And Think Like An Entrepreneur

Daily Exercises to Create the Entrepreneurial Brain!

So, let's do a little recap of what we've learned together so we can stand on solid ground and move forward. You've learned from some of the great influencers of our time and beyond. You've come to terms with how close you are to having an entrepreneurial mind or not. And you now know where you need improvement.

If you want to—and you are returning to the book after a respite—we suggest you go back over the quiz and previous chapters and refresh yourself and make some notes.

Work Book

This is where it gets fun! Here's how you use the work book. Each exercise covers one of the 15 core elements that make up the entrepreneurial mindset.

They are simple and easy to do. It's not meant to be rocket science it is only meant to habituate a pattern in your brain so you automatically start to respond naturally as an entrepreneur. It takes approximately three weeks for a new habit to form and be embedded. Although, please be aware that this is only the most common result. You may take a longer or shorter time for it to take place. There is nothing wrong with you if it takes longer. It all depends on how ingrained your way of thinking is.

Exercises

Day one Week One:

We will preface day one with this. For better time keeping, and so that you are in business mode—you should probably start this on a Monday. This way, you are going through your work week and can stay in mode the entire time and still enjoy your weekend. Some of these exercises will seem like they have nothing to do with business. Ah, but they do have everything to do with mindsets. The first week is all about conquering fears—the number one saboteur to success as an entrepreneur.

Monday:

Talk to or ask out {if you're single} someone who you perceive as "out of your league". Not in the position to date? Then talk the possibility of a business investment to some one you think would

practically laugh in your face. Even if the new idea is not real—they don't have to know that—the purpose is to dare to do something that you perceive of as great risk. Put your idea below so you are confident when you execute this exercise.

_____
_____
_____
_____

Results: Place the results below, and answer these questions.

- How did the person react?

_____
_____

- How did you feel when you approached them?

_____
_____

- What could you have done better?

_____
_____

- Was it as bad as you imagined?

_____
_____

- **Tuesday:**

Strike up a conversation that has true meaning—no small talk—with three different people. Then list three things you have in common with those people. Document the result. If you want to make it more challenging—make sure they are people you would normally be nervous to approach.

Results:

- What type of person did you talk to and why?
_____
_____

- What subjects did you bring up? And, did you stick to safe subjects or did you take more of a risk?
_____
_____

- How did that experience make you feel? Did you feel more comfortable as you went on?
_____
_____

- What three things, 9 in total did you find in common with these people?_____
_____
_____

- Could you or did you use these commonalities in a business way?
_____
_____

- **Wednesday:**

Do something physical that is well outside of your comfort zone. Dare to ignore your fear of the activity. If you perceive it as intimidating—then do it. Only you know if it's in the realm of white water rafting or bungee jumping.

But, it doesn't even have to be that extreme. It can be something on a smaller scale especially if it's in the middle of a work week. But, remember, as an entrepreneur, you'll be doing spontaneous things all the time. You aren't in the employee zone anymore.

- **Results:**

- What did you choose?_____
_____

- Why did you choose what you chose? Be honest! Did you find yourself choosing in the safe zone? And how far out of that zone did you go?

_____
_____
_____

- **Thursday:**

Find a hero. Contact a business person that you perceive as out of your league and high profile. Invite them for coffee—tell them you wanna knock some ideas around and you felt {sounding a bit unsure} that they may be able to assist them possibly.

- **Results:**

- Who did you call and why?

_____
_____

- How did they react and how did it make you feel? Did they accept the invitation? Did they rush you off the phone? Did they tell you to make an appointment with their

assistant?_____
_____
_____
_____

- What do you think you could have done better?

_____
_____
_____

- **Friday:**

Plan a road trip that will include sending yourself into a remote area. You'll want to prepare yourself for this so you aren't in danger but, you have to use your resources in order to make it through and come back alive! This is a great start to a long weekend for you!

- **Results:**

What type of plan did you come up with? How far out of the comfort zone did you go? What was the result, and what resources did you have to use?

_____
_____
_____
_____
_____
_____
_____
_____
_____

- **Monday: Day One Week Two:**

By now, you've had our variation of hell week. Only five little things that are not so little when put into practice. You know your result and should be able to fee what it's like for an entrepreneur everyday. So, if you haven't changed your mind—we can move from the physical/mental to the spiritual/mental.

Today, We want you to investigate your own spiritual philosophy and belief systems. We want you to come to terms with how strong you really feel about them and how attached you are to them. Then we can move forward.

- What spiritual philosophy do you come from?
_____
_____

- Do you consider yourself more spiritual or religious?_____
_____

- Do you follow certain religious practices if you have a family or partner at home?
_____
_____
_____

- Do you think your religious or spiritual beliefs help or hinder or would help/hinder your entrepreneurial path?

- Are you open to exploring either complimentary philosophies or completely new ones if you were sure it could help you on your entrepreneurial pathway? Yes/No and why?

- **Tuesday:**

Yesterday we made you dig a little deeply into the realm of your spirit and encouraged introspection. If it felt natural—then you are really on your way! If it felt uncomfortable—then that's great too because if you continue to place yourself out of your comfort zone—you will be that much closer to the entrepreneurial mind-set. Today we will give you a philosophy that has become popular now but has been there since the dawn of time and beyond. It has been used by the rich and world ruling 1% of the world and we are letting you in on it now. Unless you come from a very strict religious background that you are respectfully not willing to move from—this will help you greatly. It is not a religion but more of a science that can compliment any belief system. If has been praised and used by the greats. Including Albert Einstein.

- Google the Law of Attraction today. This is a law that is just as scientific as the Law of Gravity. It states that like attracts like and what we think about we bring about. Albert Einstein used it and stated-- *"Imagination is everything, it is a preview of life's coming attractions"* What it is—is Quantum Physics.

- **Results:**

- What did you learn about this new philosophy? How did it make you feel? Do you find it hard to swallow?_____
_____
_____

- Would you object to utilizing this philosophy as a test to see how it could help you? Yes/No Why?
_____
_____
_____
_____

- **Wednesday**

Today, we are so confidant you'll want to explore your spirit and the science of Quantum Physics, we have set up the rest of the week with exercises gearing you to using it. It's so simple it will seem almost crazy, but, when you use it and opportunities and what you need start to show up out of seemingly nowhere—you'll use it forever. And it is one of the best ways to really shift your thinking from a mere employee to a true entrepreneur!

- Sit quietly this morning where you won't be interrupted. Close your eyes or simply stay in bed. Think of the type of person you need to meet in order to push along this entrepreneurial life of yours. But, here is the secret about this. You have to place yourself in the 'FEELING" not just in the thought or visualization of meeting this person. You have to feel the end result. How does it FEEL to have actually met them, and how their influence helped you get what you want. Keep the "how" question out of your mind. Keep doubt as far away from you as possible. Just feel that it is done. Let it go and go about your day.

- How successful were you in keeping doubt and "how" out of your mind?

_____
_____

- Did you see any signs in your day that brought you closer to your wish? It's OK if you haven't yet. This comes with practice. You are acting as a radio transmitter to the Universe, Source or God—whatever you prefer to manifest your highest goals for you.

_____
_____
_____
_____
_____

- **Thursday:**

Look up this successful person who used this method and made it work for him. Jack Canfield and the Secret, Google it just like that and study his success story using the principles in this weeks assignments. It's always a powerful thing to find an ordinary person just like you who was making $150 bucks a week in his younger years and follow him to his greatness.

- What were your thoughts on this person and his story?_____
_____
_____
_____

- Do you see yourself in his story? What elements can you find in

him that you have already?_____
_____
_____
_____

- What elements that you find in him and his story that you would like to adopt?

_____
_____
_____
_____

- **Friday:**

Today we would like you to repeat the assignment from Thursday. We would like you to practice on small things if you've had issues trying it on big things. For example, feel what it's like to have a cup of coffee or your favorite food. Make sure you keep that joyful emotion and do this with various things and then let it go. Don't TRY to do anything. Just concentrate on the feeling once for a few minutes and let it go! Then document what you thought and any synchronizations you experienced throughout the weekend.

- Did anything that you imagined and FELT about just come to you today or over the weekend?_____
_____

- How did it make you feel? Is this a practice you are adopting with comfort?_____
_____
_____

This week was meant for you to learn to let go and at the same time to be WIDE OPEN—more than just thinking outside the box—but being open to the things that are unusual but that have helped the mega successful entrepreneurs of our time.

Monday: Week Three: Day One

Here we are going to focus on shifting your money mindset as an entrepreneur. The money mindset is the most deadly of them all and will make or break you success as an entrepreneur.

One of the most damaging beliefs about money is that you aren't worth what you charge. Today, we want you to perceive money as an exchange of energy. Like it's nothing but a tool. It goes out, it comes back and you will attract the people that can afford your services or products.

- How uncomfortable did this process make you? Why?_____
_____
_____
_____

- List 5 reasons why your product or service is worth what you are charging._____
_____
_____

- List 5 differences between you and a successful entrepreneur that does charge a premium for their services._____

_____

_____

- Is there really any difference between you and them? If so, what is it and what can you do that makes you more like them? If there is no difference, list why you still think you aren't worth it?_____

_____

_____

_____

_____

- **Tuesday**

Yesterday was quite a handful for a Monday wasn't it? We did this on purpose because by the end of the week we want you to change this deadly mindset and be selling your stuff hot! Today we are still going to address the next money and self worth issue just to make sure we've covered another side of it.

Have you felt that what you are giving others—because It may be easy for you—is not worth the price? Do you believe you are taking advantage of people or leaving the world that can't afford it to suffer without it? It's OK it means you are a 'heart entrepreneur' and there is nothing wrong with trying to help everyone. But, if you try, you'll burn out. So, we can help you balance that and at the same time—help you feel better about what you are charging and you won't be leaving many behind.

Today, start making packages for your services. Make a premium package and then for others—make stages so people can pay on a 'plan' until they are done. You don't deliver or teach until the next section is paid. Is this fair? Yes. Why? Because you are not draining your energy for very little money. You need to live too. So, you are willing to spend only so much energy with each phase of the package. If the person pulls out—you've been paid for the phases they have already been through and so it's their loss. Their lack of commitment is their issue. The premium packages will be paid for happily by those who are fully committed or who really want your package. Try it this week on a customer or two slowly to get the feel for it. Document your results

- **Results:**
- How did the process of creating a package system make you feel?_____
  _____
  _____

- How did presenting it to your customers make you feel and what were their
  reactions?_____
  _____
  _____
  _____

- Is this something you would feel comfortable with continuing? And do you view money differently?
  _____
  _____
  _____
  _____

Wednesday, Thursday, Friday:

Hopefully you are getting more comfortable with money and the worthiness of your business. Today and for the rest of the week we want you to do this. This last phase entails you writing your own entrepreneurial bio, much like the one we gave you previously. Start with I and your name and state it this way.

- I_____ am now a successful entrepreneur. I have gotten over my issues with_____. I have grown because of _____in the areas of _____. I have a strong vision of who I am and who I want to be. I am grateful to my role models_____. I emulate them in these ways_____. I know I will always be learning and I look forward to expanding myself in_____ways.

You can continue for as long as you like and keep it with you side by side with ours so you can have that inspiration always.

Conclusion

When you are starting off in anything it can be very difficult. Especially when you are trying to make a transition into something, but you don't know where to start. Hopefully this book helped you out a lot and helped you to change your mindset.

It can be hard to change your mindset especially after years and years of thinking the same way and hanging out with the wrong people whose mindsets are also wrong. It can be tough to break this pattern.

The thing that can help you is changing the people you hang out with and are friends with. If you think that your friends are not ambitious people or are not motivated and have the wrong mindset then start hanging out with different people.

Make friends with people who are more successful and are people who you want to be more like. I guarantee this will give you more success and will change your mindset for the better.

If you follow this book and actually follow the advice set out in this book it will help you become more successful. The advice contained in this book is very effective and it will help you change your mindset and fulfill your potential.

As bestselling author and motivational speaker Steve Maraboli said, 'Once your mindset changes, everything on the outside will change along with it'.

I would like to thank you for purchasing and getting to the end of this book. I appreciate you reading this book and hope you have a new changed mindset!

Be sure to check out our other books on business, marketing and entrepreneurship. You will learn how to grow your business and make more money online.

Connect with us on Facebook where we share updates, secrets, tips and tricks on business and marketing. From time to time we all giveaway free stuff including eBooks and other stuff. Follow us on Twitter as well where we also giveaway free stuff and share tips, tricks and inspirational quotes.

Also check us out on YouTube for great motivational videos, videos on increasing your time management skills and building a successful business.

Come over to www.themarketingguy.net for free resources and articles on business, entrepreneurship and marketing including tips on making money online, starting and growing your business.
Be sure to go to www.themarketingguy.net/subscribe which includes free videos, eBooks and checklists on business and entrepreneurship.

I would like to wish you all the success for you and your business. If you persevere, be consistent and never give up then your business will become a success. There is nothing that can come between you and your success!

If you found this book useful please leave a review and let me know what you think. This also lets other people easily find the book. I would highly appreciate it.

More Books from the Author

You might be interested in some of the other books that we have. Check them out:

The Success Story: Discover and Learn How Ultra Successful People Work and Achieve the Results they want

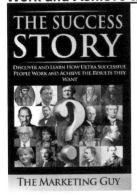

The Success Story celebrates the authors, innovators, and entrepreneurs who have become ultra-successful. We tell you what makes these entrepreneurs so special and why they are so successful. The Success Story is full of lessons that you can apply straight to your life so you can easily make your own Success Story.

We also tell you how you can replicate their success and become ultra-successful like they are. All of the entrepreneurs featured in this book have had to overcome so kind of adversity or failure but when they see the opportunity they instantly grab it.

How to Double your Traffic with Social Media: Simple Hacks To Rapidly Grow Your Fan Base

Social Media is one of the most effective ways of spreading your word out. If you use social media properly it can make your content go viral and increase your popularity and website traffic by a landslide.

If you are struggling with social media and just can't get your head around it then you need help. This guide will cover everything you wanted to know about social media.

It includes practical tips and advice on how you can instantly increase your following and fanbase on different social media channels like Facebook, Twitter, YouTube and Tumblr.

The Ultimate guide To Building an Awesome Blog: Make $1000 Passive Income a Month

When it comes to creating a blog, many people get confused and don't know what to do. You don't need to worry again.

You will learn how to set up a monthly income stream that will bring you a consistent amount of money a month.

This is a step by step guide that will tell you how to create an amazing blog. It is very simple to understand and easy to follow. It includes everything you need to know about starting your own blog and creating a successful business.

Don't Work Hard, Work Smart: Tools, Apps and Resources that Every Blogger and Entrepreneur Should Use (That Are Completely Free and Awesome)

Discover The Exact Business, Productivity & Marketing Tools Today's Highly Successful Entrepreneurs and Businesses Use! This book features completely FREE tools that will help you grow your business and take it to the next level.

These aren't just your normal crap tools that you can find anywhere. These are used by top successful entrepreneurs like Tim Ferriss, Seth Godin, Guy Kawasaki and Pat Flynn to name a few.

There are hundreds of tools, resources and apps featured in this book that are from tons of categories from FREE productivity tools to FREE customer relationship management tools. This book would easily save you time and energy as well saving potentially saving you hundreds and hundreds of dollars.

How to Start A Business with Practically No Money: Become An Entrepreneur and Build a Successful and Profitable Business

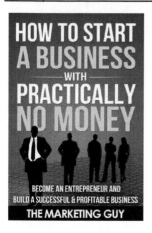

This guide has everything covered on making money online and building and growing your own business. In this book you will learn:

- Why you NEED to build your own business
- What you need to do to become a successful entrepreneur
- How to get that amazing business idea
- Why Failure is a good thing
- Business ideas that you can implement TODAY to start making money straight away

The book contains much more and this is just a little sample of what you will learn.

Printed in Great Britain
by Amazon.co.uk, Ltd.,
Marston Gate.